2019
Uncle Andy
&
Aunt Jen

The Story of
ISAMBARD KINGDOM BRUNEL

The Story of

ISAMBARD KINGDOM BRUNEL
The Man Who Built Britain

———————

By Amanda Mitchison

First published as *Who Was... Isambard Kingdom Brunel*
in 2006 by Short Books
Unit 316, ScreenWorks,
22 Highbury Grove
London N5 2ER

This hardback edition published as part of the "Great Victorians"
series in 2017 by Short Books

10 9 8 7 6 5 4 3 2 1

A CIP catalogue record for this book is available
from the British Library.

ISBN 978-1-78072-325-9

Cover illustrations © Evie Dunne
Cover design by Daniella Shreir

Printed in Great Britain by CPI Group (UK) Ltd,
Croydon, CR0 4YY

To Duncan Barrington

CHAPTER ONE
The Worm

Marc Brunel sat in his study in London on an autumn morning. His head was full of mathematical equations and designs for bridges and knitting machines. But his desk was covered in accounts which he was ignoring as very best he could. His window looked out onto the River Thames at the bottom of the garden, and, over the muddy water on the far bank, he could see his ruinous sawmill at Battersea.

As is only proper for a man of towering genius, Marc Brunel lives on the verge of ruin. His sawmill was the talk of London – his miraculous machines could cut mahogany into slices as thin as ham – but it was a financial disaster. Until recently he had also possessed a factory to supply the army with boots. But then came the battle of Waterloo in 1815, which put an end not only to Napoleon Bonaparte, but also to Brunel's factory. For with peace in Europe nobody now needed soldiers. Marc Brunel was left holding 80,000 pairs of soldiers' boots.

Boots!

Marc Brunel gave a shudder and stared out of the window. A small dark-haired boy of eleven was running full pelt along the back garden wall. Marc Brunel tapped on the glass and beckoned.

A minute later there was a knock on the door. In came the boy, with a large scroll of paper under his arm. His trousers were covered in mud, and water dripped onto the carpet.

"Your hair is wet again, Isambard!" exclaimed Marc Brunel.

"Yes, papa. I took a swim before breakfast. The water is capital! The current pulls like a dray horse," announced the boy eagerly.

"You'll catch a chill. Have you taken your rhubarb?"

"I have indeed, papa," replied Isambard, opening the scroll onto the desk. "And could you kindly look at my plans? As you suggested, I have been making a survey of Hove. But please do lend me your long measure. I need it to make the elevations more exact."

8

Marc Brunel looked down at his son's work and smiled. The architectural drawings were beautiful, a masterpiece of precision and elegance with "fecit Isambard Kingdom Brunel, 1817" written in a fine copperplate hand in one corner.

The boy always seemed to have inky fingers and little bits of balsa wood in his hair, yet his paperwork appeared so very elegant and effortless. And so it should have been. Marc Brunel had given his son drawing lessons from the age of four and had made him practise till he could draw a perfect circle freehand.

Marc Brunel examined the plans more closely then shut his eyes to remember the sea front at Hove, where Isambard was attending a boarding school.

"If you must add peacocks, get the plumage right." Marc Brunel didn't like fancifulness.

"Yes, papa."

"And I see you have added two porticos here."

Brunel jabbed a finger at the plans.

"Yes, I thought that an improvement," said Isambard breezily. "And you'll notice some Moorish columns to the West of the esplanade."

"Beware of overconfidence, Isambard. You know great things are expected from you."

"Yes, papa," replied Isambard. The boy turned the handle of a small box on his father's desk. The box made a gentle whirring noise – it was a card-shuffling machine that Marc Brunel had just devised for a friend.

Marc Brunel clicked his fingers to regain his son's attention.

"You've done well with your drawings – I have always said that surveys are an engineer's alphabet, but how are your studies in mathematics?"

"We are on proposition 27 of the Elements," replied Isambard. "We've completed postulates of construction."

"Commensurable and incommensurable magnitudes?" asked Marc Brunel softly.

"Not yet, papa."

"Hmm", murmured Marc Brunel. "We should take the air, boy." It was a while since he had tested the boy's power of observation.

Isambard jumped down the stairs three at a time. His father descended at a more measured pace.

Outside they took the road west along the Embankment. The elm trees arched overhead, and the River Thames slithered by their side. Isambard hopscotched his way along the pavement. Suddenly he stopped and pointed to a new building under construction on the other side of the road.

"I would not venture near that building, papa!"

"Why do you say so, boy?" asked Marc Brunel.

"The load is all wrong!" exclaimed Isambard. "It can't stay up, papa. Look at the curvature of that arch! And that wall is all awry. Look how it bulges so!"

"Anything else?" prompted Marc Brunel. He hoped the boy had also examined the brickwork.

"The finishing is poor, papa. And I'd wager the mortar be badly mixed."

"So what do you say? Two weeks?"

"Maybe three, papa."

Marc Brunel rubbed his chin and looked up at the sky. The air had a yellowish tinge to it, for autumn was drawing in. "No. I would say sooner. Always remember to take account of the weather. If there's heavy rain, that wall will be down by the morning." And, despite himself, Marc Brunel smiled. There was always something satisfying about a bad building falling down.

Marc Brunel rummaged in his waistcoat pocket and brought out a cotton handkerchief.

"Now, my child," said Brunel. "Let me show you my new idea."

He crouched down and unfolded the handkerchief. Isambard peered into his father's cupped hands
– there lay a strange creature with a long, white
tendril-like body and a larger, black head. The thing
was clearly dead. It smelt of the sea.

"Is it from an octopus?"

"No child. Feel it."

Isambard prodded. The body seemed soft, but the
head was hard, as if it had a crust.

"Teredo navalis", said Marc Brunel quietly. "Ship's
worm. It burrows into wood. Isambard, look at the
head, where it gnaws away."

And Isambard looked closer. The black head was
made up of several interlocking pieces of shell.

"You see? They are shields. Think of that. Now
think of the River Neva at St Petersburg. Every year
the river freezes over and the ice floes carry away the
piers of the bridges. So what do you need to cross the
bridge?"

"A tunnel, papa", replied Isambard.

"Precisely! But to build an underwater tunnel you
need to support the structure as you go. How do you
do it? You do what the worm does. You burrow with
shields to protect yourself." Marc Brunel placed the
handkerchief back into his pocket and, as he did so,

Isambard's face crumpled slightly with disappointment.

"This time", added Marc Brunel in a determined voice, "I will remember to patent my invention."

"Papa?" Isambard slipped his hand into his father's. Brunel smiled down at him. This child's power of observation were remarkable, quite remarkable.

"May I keep that worm?"

CHAPTER TWO
The Tunnel

Marc Brunel had great hopes for his son, but he knew that the boy needed good quadratic equations and plenty of practice with a lathe and a chisel. So, at the age of fourteen, he sent Isambard off to France to attend two schools renowned for their teaching of mathematics. The boy also served as an apprentice with Louis Breguet, a famous watchmaker and an exquisite craftsman.

This time in France gave Isambard Brunel exacting standards and a taste for rather grandiose architecture. It also meant he missed out on a most unpleasant family experience. In 1821, after years of financial difficulty, Marc Brunel was finally declared bankrupt. He and his wife Sophia spent three months in debtor's prison, until influential friends prevailed upon the government to grant him £5,000 to clear his debts.

By 1822, when the sixteen-year-old Isambard returned to England, Marc Brunel had set up office again and needed an assistant. So he set his son to work. Over the next four years, Isambard Brunel designed a treadmill for a gaol and a mausoleum; he made a land survey from Fowey to Padstow in Cornwall; and helped with designs for a Dutch canon-boring mill, a rotary printing press, and a canal at Panama. He worked on a floating pier and swing bridge for Liverpool dock, a saw mill in British Guiana, and also fitted in half a dozen suspension bridges.

But these jobs were small fry compared with what was to come. A far bigger, harder, dirtier project awaited Isambard. This would mark his coming of age as an engineer and very nearly cost him his life. And it all derived from that ship's worm his father had shown him eight years earlier.

When Marc Brunel had first noticed the hard shells on the ship worm's head, he had designed a tunnelling shield – a contraption that would hold earth in place while a tunnel was excavated. Finally he found an outlet for this daring idea. In 1824, Marc Brunel was appointed chief engineer of the Thames Tunnel Company. He was to build a tunnel from Wapping, on the North bank of the Thames, to Rotherhithe, on the South bank. At that time no one had ever succeeded in building a tunnel under a river before.

On 2 March, 1825, Marc Brunel laid down the first brick and Isambard the second brick and then church bells rang and 200 dignitaries sat down to a sumptuous meal with a model of the tunnel in sugar in the middle of the table. By November that year the shaft down to the tunnel had been completed. Now it was time for Brunel's shields to get to work.

The shields – there were twelve of them – were as huge and cumbersome as mammoths. Each one was 21 feet high (almost seven metres), with a great metal plate to hold up the roof of the tunnel and three separate compartments, one on top of the other, so that three men could dig at the same time. Against the face of the tunnel lay a series of heavy, horizontal oak planks held in place with screws. The men would remove one plank at a time, dig away a few inches of earth and then, having extended the screw deeper into the tunnel, replace the plank. When all the planks had been moved to their extended position, the entire frame would be moved forward and bricklayers would fill in the tunnel wall. Then the whole process would begin again, and the twelve lumbering mammoths would slowly tunnel their way under the Thames inch by inch. That was the theory.

But it was filthy work. Geologists had assured Marc Brunel that the shield would be burrowing through solid clay. This was not true. At times only gravel separated the tunnel from the river above. Water and raw sewage poured in through the staves, sand blocked the pumps, everywhere seemed to ooze out noxious black mud sprinkled with bones and old crockery. The stench was overpowering. The workmen's fingernails rotted away, they suffered attacks of vomiting and dizziness. They caught "tunnel fever", a mysterious infection which caused sudden blindness and sometimes death.

The men were caught between fire and water. They worked under gas light and they knew there was marsh gas* in the tunnel that could explode at any moment. Meanwhile, above them loomed the River Thames, which was always threatening to roar down into the tunnel and drown them all. The water washed its way constantly into the men's boots and into their nightmares. And the Irish labourers, who

* Words marked with an asterix are explained in the glossary on page 99

17

were fearful and fanciful men, believed that only the darkness would save them. Whenever there was a rush of water they put out all their lamps. That way, so they hoped, the water wouldn't find them. This made repairs all the harder.

Marc Brunel, who was in his fifties, didn't have the constitution for underground work and came down with pleurisy* shortly after the tunnelling began. A few months later, the resident engineer William Armstrong was unable to take the strain and resigned. This left Isambard Brunel, only twenty years old, to oversee what was then the world's most daring engineering project.

And so it was that at five o'clock on the morning of 14 January, 1828, Brunel woke up on a small wooden platform down in the depths of the tunnel. He leapt to his feet and gave himself a quick shake, like a dog emerging from water.

Refreshed by just half an hour's sleep, he turned and cast an eye over the great shields behind him – water was hissing through the planks, but when they were so near the bed of the river that was to be expected. At least the brickwork did not seem to be swelling.

Brunel strode back along the tunnel to the workers'

staircase and, lighting his cigar as he went, he thought angrily about the Thames Tunnel Company. He was on a mere £200 a year – and his parents were still too pinched for money to keep a butler, let alone a carriage and horses. He had risked his neck countless times for the company. Only six months ago there had been a terrible breach in the river bed, and water had roared down the tunnel, and everyone had had to run for their lives. But it was Brunel who had gone back down into the darkness with a rope to haul an old engine man to safety.

Afterwards, when the tunnel was patched up and cleared, he had organised an underground banquet for these same stingy, cheeseparing company directors and it had been a splendid affair with candelabra and crimson banners and a brass band of Coldstream Guards playing deafeningly. And had Brunel not spent hours accompanying dignatories round the tunnel? Why, only three days ago Don Miguel, the pretender to the throne of Portugal, had been down examining the shields.

Brunel ran up the workmen's staircase into the early morning light. (There was a separate visitors' staircase. Despite the dangers, the Thames Tunnel Company had opened the tunnel to public viewing at a shilling a head.) He pushed open the door into the little office at the head of the shaft where his assistant, Richard Beamish, was signing out dockets for gin and warm beer to give to the night shift. Beamish wrote with his head tilted slightly to one side – he had lost an eye to tunnel fever.

Brunel looked at himself in the small mirror by the jug in the corner. Because he was so fearful of another collapse of the tunnel, he had been on the job for days and nights on end. And it showed. His linen was a disgrace. He splashed a little water on his face, and wiped away the black deposit that had formed round his nostrils. Then he raked a hand through his curly hair, grabbed his bowler hat and walked out into the sunlight.

The morning shift were standing ready for inspection. Brunel walked along the line of men, holding his cigar behind his back, so that he could smell their breath as he passed them. The worst drunks had been fired long ago, but steadier men also sometimes forgot themselves.

Brunel stopped in front of a bricklayer with a cap squashed down over his eyes. The young man was swaying slightly from side to side. Brunel inhaled – the gin fumes made his eyes water.

"Price!" he exclaimed, "By Jove, you're combustible! If you can't stand straight, you surely can't build a wall. Go home man!"

Price, with his eyes smouldering, slouched off. Later, he would thank Brunel from his heart for having turned him away that day.

Down in the tunnel the little gas lights flickered in the darkness. Brunel stood behind frame Number One and watched the gigantic shadows of two of his very best miners, Collins and Ball, reflected on the huge, arching wall. It might smell terrible down here, and be bitterly cold, but the tunnel did look spectacular. Brunel made a mental note: "I must make some India ink sketches."

Brunel took out his pocket watch. It was six o'clock now, and the tide in the Thames Estuary was at its very highest. This meant that directly overhead lay 600 tons of water. God spare them!

"Sir!" cried Collins. "Sir!"

Brunel looked over to where the men had been removing side shores from frame Number One. The side of the tunnel wall was moving!

"Replace the planks directly!" shouted Brunel.

Ball and Collins started to screw back the missing

staves, but already the wall was bellying in towards them. Suddenly the bricks gave way and a great column of water rose up from the ground. After a terrible pause, it crashed down, sweeping Collins and Ball off the frame and pulling down the wooden platform where Brunel had been standing.

The gas lights went out and now there was just darkness and screams of terror as the torrent of freezing water bore down on them. Brunel spluttered to the surface and as he did so a barrel of cement smashed into his side. He came up again, gasping like a fish. But his leg was caught under a joist from the collapsed platform.

The water was rushing round his waist now and trying to pull him down. Brunel tugged at his left leg. He pulled and twisted, but felt the wood settle heavier on the leg. If he didn't get out soon the water would be round his neck. Or maybe the frame would come down on him and kill him first.

He clutched his thigh with both hands, and, using all his might, he yanked at his leg. Ahh! This time he felt the joist move. He pulled again. His leg was free now.

In the darkness Brunel started to wade through the water towards the shaft.

"Ball, Collins! Come! This way!" But his voice sounded small against the roar of the water.

He pushed on into the darkness. He couldn't feel the knee that had been trapped – something was broken but that hardly mattered as long as he could stagger on.

In fact he couldn't feel much at all – all he knew was that he must get to the shaft. And where were Ball and Collins? The water pressure was building in the tunnel. A great wave would come soon and pull them all down.

"Ball! Collins!" he cried. But there was no reply.

When Brunel reached the head of the shaft, the stairs were blocked by throngs of men swearing and screaming and trying to scramble over each other to get out.

Brunel turned away from the crowd. This was no good – far better to try the visitor's stairs. He made for the opening between the two arches of the tunnel and when he reached the foot of the visitor's stairway he stopped. Where were his men?

"Ball! Collins!" he cried. "Ball! Collins! This way! Ball! Collins!"

Brunel went on calling out into the darkness until the great surge of water enveloped him.

Up in his little office Richard Beamish was still making out dockets when the watchman burst in crying, "The water is in! The tunnel is full!"

Beamish ran to the workmen's stairway, but his way was blocked by the desperate men pushing to escape. Beamish rushed to the visitor's entrance, smashed the door down with a crowbar and ran to the stairway.

He had only started down the steps when the water roared up to meet him. A terrible sight met his eyes. There, face down on the crest of the wave, was the still body of Isambard Brunel. As the wave came towards him, Beamish reached out, grabbed his master by the back of his jacket and hauled him back up the steps.

Beamish put Brunel down on the ground, and there he lay with his leg bleeding and river water sluicing out of his mouth. Every so often he murmured, "Ball, Collins…"

Ball and Collins never did make it back to the surface, and four other men also died in the accident. But later that morning Brunel, having regained consciousness, returned to work. He could barely speak and was too injured to sit up, but he had the mattress he was lying on carried out onto a barge. He wanted his men to survey the river bottom in a diving bell and find out the extent of the damage immediately. "There is," he croaked, "no time to waste."

CHAPTER THREE
The Bridge

Brunel took a long time to recover from his accident. As well as damaging his leg, he had internal injuries and spent several days in bed until his doctors announced he was well enough to go down to Brighton on the south coast to convalesce.

But Brighton was a gay, bustling place and Brunel overdid the theatre visits and the fancy dress balls. One night, after riding a horse, he started to bleed violently inside. Faithful Beamish was sent to bring him home and this time he was confined to bed for several months.

Eventually, Brunel was allowed to leave London. It was decided he should not return to Brighton, but go somewhere which was quieter and had fewer actresses. So instead Brunel went to Plymouth and then on to Bristol, where he frequented Clifton, the smart part of the city that rests on the cliffs above the Avon Gorge. Here Brunel became a familiar sight. In the winter of 1828, local residents could look over the edge of the terrifyingly steep gorge and see a small man with a tall bowler hat and an enormous Meerschaum cigar, clambering around the escarpment with a sketch book under his arm.

For Brunel was, as usual, busy. A competition to design a bridge across the Avon Gorge had been announced. Brunel worked like a fiend, and went to Wales to inspect Thomas Telford's new Menai suspension bridge, which, with a central span of 580 feet, was then the longest bridge in the world.

On the closing date of the competition Brunel submitted four different, beautifully drawn designs for bridges. Brunel's proposed bridges were all gothically extravagant and at least some 300 feet longer than the Menai suspension bridge. In order to counter wind resistance, Brunel had reinforced his bridges with transverse braces and had used extremely short suspension rods at the centre of the span, bringing the chains down almost to the level of the road.

Thomas Telford, who was then 70 years old, was called in by the judges to examine the entries and he rejected them all. Brunel's bridges, he claimed, were too long. He rules that the maximum safe span for a suspension bridge was 600 feet, which happened to be just twenty feet more than his Menai Bridge.

A second competition was held. Brunel altered one of his original designs, reducing the span to 630 feet and adding an "Egyptian" theme, with two great monolithic towers at either end of the bridge and four sphinxes looking out over the gorge.

Again Brunel's entry was rejected. But he was not to be outdone. And he knew that nobody could be more compelling on the subject of suspension rods and the relative merits of single and double pins. So he called a meeting with the Clifton Suspension Bridge Committee, and here he talked the judges through his calculations until they obeyed and took on his design.

Afterwards, on the morning of 21st June, 1831, a ceremony was held to mark the beginning of work on the Clifton Suspension Bridge. A band of dragoon guards at the bottom of the gorge played the National Anthem, flags were raised, there was champagne for the ladies and gentlemen and a barrel of beer for the workers, and much raucous cheering and roaring of cannon. A local dignitary gave a flowery speech in which he called the bridge-to-be "the ornament of Bristol and the wonder of the age".

But all this fanfare was tempting fate. Soon problems arose. The Bridge Committee found it was short of funds; there were legal wrangles; and after three months, riots over parliamentary reform reduced Bristol to complete chaos. The wonder of the age was promptly shelved.

During this period Brunel had little luck with his other projects. The Thames tunnel had been bricked up after the flood and it would be another seven years before work was resumed and by then Isambard Brunel would no longer be involved. There was also the great disappointment of the "Gaz machine", which was erected in the abandoned offices of the Thames tunnel and was probably the Brunels' longest running and most expensive white elephant.

The Gaz machine, originally dreamed up by Marc Brunel, was to be the new, cheap alternative to the steam engine. The idea, put very simply, was to heat up a mixture of sulphuric acid and carbonate of ammonia, and then harness the energy from the very high pressure levels created by the resulting gases. Isambard Brunel spent years and about £15,000 devising hideously dangerous machinery to carry out this task. Somehow he never managed to blow himself to bits. In 1833, he finally abandoned the project for good.

Isambard Brunel tendered for other work. He was commissioned to construct a new dock at Monk-wearmouth in Sunderland, but his first designs were rejected by parliament. He drew up surveys for a new dry dock in Woolwich for the Navy, but this came to nothing.

He applied for the post of engineer on England's first coast-to-coast railway – the Newcastle to Carlisle line – but the post went to someone else. The one job Brunel did accomplish – an observatory with a revolving dome for the astronomer Sir James South – went three times over budget, led to furious arguments and an anonymous magazine article which lambasted Brunel and called the observatory "absurd".

But still Brunel persevered, travelling up and down the country on coaches as he searched for work. He wanted to be independent of his parents now and when he was in London he often stayed with his lively older sister Sophia, whose husband Benjamin Hawes became perhaps his dearest friend. Brunel also had a quieter sister Emma, but little is known of her except that she was prone to nervous headaches, married a curate and died young.

Brunel wanted the good life. He wanted a beautiful, accomplished wife, a carriage and horses, liveried footmen or, at the very least, servants in gloves. But he did sometimes wonder: Would he have to settle for some mediocre job, with a snug little wife in a snug little house? He chafed as his contemporaries flourished. John Rennie's magnificent London Bridge was opened by King William IV (Queen Victoria's uncle) in 1831; Henry Palmer was building the New London Dock, and George and Robert Stephenson were forging ahead with the first railways.

And what did Brunel have under his belt? An incomplete tunnel, an unbuilt bridge, the useless Gaz engine, two floundering dock schemes... For some time he felt everything he tried to grab at was slipping by him, as if the pig's tail were soaped.

Then, all of a sudden, Brunel seemed inundated with jobs. In 1833 he started the gargantuan task of surveying the land for a railway line from London to Bristol and soon appointments as chief engineer on other railways began to rain down on him. He also worked on a scheme to improve the docks and clear mud from the waterways in Bristol.

In addition, Brunel had agreed to be engineer for the Hungerford Suspension Bridge. And it wasn't very long before he was even collaborating with friends on what many at the time considered to be a madcap idea – designing a steam ship that could cross the Atlantic. In April 1836 he totted up his bewildering number of jobs in his diary and wrote "really my business is something extraordinary".

So, now that Brunel was professionally established, he could be as extravagant as he wished. One of his most expensive acquisitions was a wife. On 5 July, 1836, he married the very beautiful and haughty Mary Horsley. She was the opposite of a snug little wife and it does not seem to have been a very close marriage. Brunel was so busy he was hardly ever at home.

But, for Mary, there were compensations for his absences. She got a fine house and enormous billowing crinolines. She had a carriage lined with green silk for day-time use and one in cream silk for the evenings. She never took a stroll in the park without a footman in livery following behind. On Sundays, just in case the spirit moved her, a servant would carry her ivory and gilt clasped prayer book.

After a brief honeymoon, the Brunels went to

Bristol for the reopening of work on the Clifton Suspension Bridge – for enough money had finally been raised to get construction of the bridge underway.

On the morning of 27th August, 1836, crowds lined both sides of the cliffs, and ships with their flags up thronged the River Avon. When the Marquis of Northampton laid the foundation stone, the crowds cheered and the trumpeters sounded a fanfare. The echo reverberated far down the gorge.

Work began on the bridge. The first thing needed was some means for carrying men and materials from one side of the gorge to the other. So Brunel ordered the men to weld together a wrought iron rod, one thousand feet long. The rod would straddle the top of the gorge and from this rod a sturdy basket would be suspended on a roller. Using ropes, the basket would then be pulled back and forth across the gorge.

The first rod was a failure. While it was being fixed in place it slipped its moorings and fell down into the river bed with an almighty crash. Eventually it was hoisted back out of the mud and put in place. But by now the rod had a small kink in the middle and when the first man attempted the crossing, the roller got stuck in this kink, and the ropes became entangled on the mast of a passing ship and the man very, very nearly plummeted to his death.

Brunel had been busy on one of his other countless projects at the time and when he heard what had happened, he was furious. How dare they go ahead without his express permission! If anyone was going to be the first person to wobble through the skies in a souped-up laundry basket it would be him. And he would be accompanied – if he could only work on her – by the new Mrs Brunel.

A month later, when a new rod was fitted, Brunel stood on the escarpment looking down 200 feet to the river bed where tiny men were watering tiny horses. He took his cigar out of his mouth and stuck it out into the air, as if he was hailing a hansom* cab with it. The smoke blew directly towards Bristol. Ahha! Just as he thought. The wind was coming from the east, no doubt gathering speed as it came down the gorge. In the basket he would have the opportunity to experience the violent air currents at first hand, and that would be most interesting.

Brunel turned to his wife Mary, who was looking the picture of elegance in a lilac silk skirt and dove grey mantle. She knew from her bonnet ribbons that it was a very gusty day.

"Come, my dear. You'll enjoy it! It will be a grand event. The view will be capital!"

Mary gripped very firmly on the metal rail and peered over the gorge. Down below lay the deep brown mud of the river bank. That would be if she was lucky – nearer to hand were the jagged rocks of the limestone escarpment. She shut her eyes. How could he even think of it! But her new husband wouldn't understand. She had already noticed how much he enjoyed danger.

Seeing her pale face, Brunel added, "Wicker work is very sturdy."

"Well yes," replied Mary Brunel quietly, "but very snagging."

She watched the men hoisting the basket onto a small cement pier on the cliff face. The sides of the basket were a metre high. Apart from the small matter of certain death, there was also the question of propriety.

She would have to – oh, the horror of it! – clamber into this contraption. What about her petticoats! And her ankles! And with the labourers watching!

Mary Brunel turned to her husband. "And how precisely do you suggest I should get into this contraption?"

"Oh, we'll get a boy to bring some library steps," replied Brunel.

Mary Brunel shuddered, "Mr Brunel, I don't think that would be at all ladylike."

Brunel sighed. Then he turned and walked over to a group of men in frock coats who were standing by the edge of the gorge. Brunel found his friend Captain Christopher Claxton and said "I'll take the lad then."

Claxton beckoned to his son William.

"Oh yes! Yes! If you please!" exclaimed young Master Claxton.

Captain Claxton ruffled the boy's hair. "Mind your manners, William."

"Oh I will, papa! I will."

The basket had two wooden shelves that served as seats at either end. Brunel sat with his back to the gorge, with William facing him. The boy grinned and wriggled and waved to his father.

"Hold tight!" said Brunel, and he nodded to the workmen to release the catch.

With a lurch and a screech from the rollers, the basket set off skidding down the rod, going faster and faster and faster. Soon they were well out over the gorge, with the roller squeaking and the wind buffeting the basket from side to side. Little William was no longer grinning. Brunel held onto his top hat and looked down at the great, brown snake of the River Avon. It was tempting to lean out even further over the side. Indeed, the river seemed to want to pull you towards it. If he stretched out his arm now he could almost touch the back of a gull.

Suddenly, when they had reached the very middle of the gorge, the rollers slammed to a halt, rocking the basket violently to and fro. The boy let out a scream and Brunel cursed under his breath. He looked up at the iron rod, which was slightly bowed under the weight of the basket. The rollers attaching the basket to the rod were again stuck in that small kink.

"Hold on, boy!"

Brunel threw his cigar down into the river, put his hat on the seat and, though the basket was still lurching to and fro, he stood up. He clutched hold of the ropes and started to rock his weight back and forth.

Maybe a sudden movement would jerk the rollers back into action. The boy looked on appalled.

But it was no good. The rollers were still stuck. There was nothing for it. Nobody else could save them. Either they sat here until they perished of cold and hunger, or he had to go up. The dangerousness of what he was about to do gave him a strange sense of calm. Brunel smiled reassuringly to young William.

"Hold my hat, young man and sit down on the floor to keep us steady."

Then, with the boy crouching between the seats, Brunel grasped the rope in both hands and started to hoist himself up. The climb was slow. Brunel inched his way up the rope, bit by bit, with the rope burning his hands and the wind slapping against his face. Every time he pulled upwards, the basket below him seemed to lurch further from side to side. Eventually he reached the iron rod.

If the basket were to move at all, he now needed to release the pressure on the rollers. So, with his feet still round the rope, he held onto the iron bar with his right hand and rested his weight there. There was, he knew, nothing between him and the gorge.

With the other hand he tried to move the rollers along the rod. Nothing happened. If only he had some oil with him – the rollers simply needed lubricating. He tried a second time and still nothing happened. Then he clutched the rope again with two hands, shut his eyes, and breathed deeply for a moment.

He would try once more. He grasped the rod

again with his right hand, swung his weight across and then, holding his breath with the effort, pushed against the rollers. This time something squeaked and slowly the mechanism creaked forwards. Finally they were free!

Brunel slid gently down the rope and into the basket, where William was crouched on the ground with his head in his hands. He had not felt able to watch Brunel's feat of gymnastics.

But standing on the edge a small figure in lavender and grey had seen every dreadful minute of the escapade. As the basket moved off towards the far side of the gorge, Mary Brunel twiddled her parasol and pursed her lips in annoyance. They really were going to have to come to an understanding.

CHAPTER FOUR
The Railway

When Brunel became engineer for the Great Western Railway, he envisioned – as he so often did – something far greater than anything that had gone before.

Until then railways had been relatively small scale affairs, principally for moving goods over quite short distances. But the Great Western Railway was a different matter altogether.

This line was to join Bristol and London, which were then two of the biggest commercial centres in England. And it wouldn't just be for freight, it would be principally for passengers to sit back in comfort and drink their coffee at the then unthinkable speed of 45 miles an hour. In order to be this fast, the line had to be straight. It was not to curve round the sides of hills, it would go through them. It was not to wind down into valleys, it would fly straight over them suspended on viaducts.

And, of course, Bristol to London was only the beginning. This was to be the first trunk line – soon there would be branches off to Oxford, Exeter, Newport... The possibilities were infinite.

The task was gargantuan. First Brunel had to survey the land, riding on horseback by day as he examined the lie of the ground and then, in the evening settling down to paper work, staying up most of the night hours pouring over plans, writing up reports and letters and doing his calculations. In order to save time, he had a special horse-drawn, black carriage made for himself with a bed, a drawing board, and fitted cupboards for all his drawings and surveying equipment. Inside there was also, of course, a neatly built-in box to hold his beloved cigars. Eventually, Brunel chose a route following the Thames valley west out of London, then taking the grassy uplands of the White Horse Vale, going through Chippenham, swooping down through Box Hill into Bath and then passing through the Avon valley into Bristol. He hadn't stinted on the engineering works. For example, Box Hill would require a two-mile tunnel, half a mile of which had to be blasted out of solid rock, and Bath station was elevated and approached by a viaduct of 73 arches.

Before this railway could be built, it needed to be approved by a bill through parliament, and for that bill to pass, Great Western Railways needed to have public support and funding. So, on his journeys, Brunel was addressing public meetings and trying to win over local landowners who might not fancy a railway line going through their land. Brunel hated this aspect of the job and it was impossible to make everybody happy.

A certain Reverend Proctor Thomas of Wellington was furious that one of Brunel's embankments would mean the end of his fish pond, and the public school Eton College opposed the railway because the masters didn't want their boys getting to London easily where they could be corrupted. Meanwhile, the people in Windsor complained that the line did not come near enough to the town.

Eventually, on the second attempt, the bill was passed by parliament. In 1835 work could start on the line. Brunel did everything. He formulated the accountancy system, he wrote the draft contracts for every job, he scrutinised the legal documents, he checked all the accounts, and he even researched which species of grass should be grown on the railway sidings. He wanted to control everything and everybody and never believed others could do as well as himself.

On such a gigantic project as the railway this was clearly going to cause problems. Brunel spent years travelling up and down the line in his special carriage, working twenty hours a day, taking occasional naps in his armchair (often with his cigar in his mouth) and forever sending off angry little notes to his subordinates. As he ignored his birthdays and worked straight through weekends and barely saw his wife, he expected others to do likewise. He was what people call "an exacting employer", which really means that he was a nightmare to work for.

And Brunel, of course, designed everything – from the bridges and the viaducts and the stations, down to the signals and the cross bars. His style was graceful and austere, but still quite grandiose. The entrances to the box tunnel between Chippenham and Bath are framed by great porticos, Temple Meads Station in Bristol has turrets, and the basic structure of Paddington station is three great towering curves of glass and metal, similar to Joseph Paxton's Crystal Palace built for the Great Exhibition of 1851.

Brunel had also designed his own track. At the time railways were made of cast iron which was an unsuitable material for a load-bearing beam. Rolled, wrought iron was far stronger, but during the cooling process it was liable to split open and become uneven. To solve this problem Brunel invented an inverted "U" shaped wrought iron track which, because it cooled more evenly than a solid bar, was less likely to distort and was also lighter and cheaper.

Other inventions were less successful. Brunel experimented with different ways of bedding the track in the ground and the original specifications he gave the locomotive makers meant that his first trains were underpowered, with boilers that were far too small. Brunel had also – and this in the end was to be his biggest mistake – insisted on using a new gauge of railway. On other railways, the gauge (that means the width between the rails in the ground and therefore the distance between the wheels of the trains) was four feet and eight-and-a-half inches. Brunel decided to broaden the gauge to seven feet. Later, when the railway network throughout the county began to link up, this was to cause enormous problems.

But while the railway was being built, Brunel had many other far more pressing concerns. In his diaries he wrote of the "swarm of little devils" that beset him, "leaky pickle-tanks, uncut timber, half finished station houses, sinking embankments, broken screws, absent guard plates, unfinished drawings and sketches."

Contractors went bankrupt, there were perpetual wranglings with local landowners, the early loco-motives were a disaster, some of the track had to be completely relaid, the bridge over the Thames at Maidenhead showed signs of sagging, and there were divisions within the board of the Great Western Railway. In 1837 Brunel's opponents made a concerted effort to gain greater control. But Brunel held his nerve and won the battle.

There was, however, one problem that Brunel took years to resolve. When the first section of the railway – from Paddington to Maidenhead – finally opened in June 1838, it soon became clear that nobody was going to be sipping their coffee as the train purred along at 45 miles an hour. For when the trains went fast, the ride was rough. The wheels made a loud, thumping noise and the carriages swayed horribly from side to side. Brunel couldn't understand why. When he rode on the trains, he would stand on the footboard and move along the outside, jumping from carriage to carriage looking for faults. At the stations he would often be seen crawling around under the locomotives. It wasn't until 1842 that he finally discovered the cause of the thumping – an inequality in the thickness of the tyres which was throwing the wheels out of balance.

Other problems arose. During the terrible winter of 1839 the chairman of the Great Western company shot himself. Meanwhile, torrential rains drowned the valleys of the Thames and Avon, making the water-logged clay slide down the embankments and reducing everything to a quagmire. At Sonning Hill, between Reading and Twyford, where a 60-foot cutting was being hewn through the soil, conditions were terrible and, after two contractors gave up, Brunel took control using 1,220 navvies and 196 horses to move the earth.

But nothing was as hard and dangerous as the cutting of the monstrously ambitious two-mile tunnel through Box Hill, just outside Bath. For two and a half years the work consumed a ton of gunpowder and a ton of candles every week. A hundred workmen perished under Box Hill and on the day the two ends of the tunnel finally met – the workmen had been digging from both ends of the hill – Brunel was so pleased and relieved that he took the ring from his finger and gave it to the foreman.

The Chippenham to Bath section of the line was the hardest part of the Great Western railway and the last to be completed. But finally, on 30 June, 1841, a decorated train pulled out of Paddington and arrived four hours later in Bristol. The Great Western Railway line, 116 miles from Bristol to London, had taken eight years to build and cost £6,500,000, which was nearly three times Brunel's original estimate and about £429 million in today's money.

There was still plenty to do – stations, and workshops, and further extensions – but the line was now up and running. Brunel was only 35 and he had completed probably the greatest of all his engineering works. And, just for once, he had managed to finish a major project without almost breaking his neck. He would have to wait another two years for his next brush with death.

CHAPTER FIVE
The Coin

By 1843 Brunel was rich and famous. And, although he was almost never there, he loved the plush home that he and Mary had made for themselves at 18 Duke Street, backing onto St James's Park in the middle of London. He loved their Dresden china and their crimson silk curtains, their Venetian glass mirrors, their wood panelling and Christmas cake plaster work. He loved their extraordinary collection of weighty silverware: the tankards, soup tureens, the great domed platters which kept their fried kidneys warm for Sunday breakfast and could fell a burglar stone dead with one blow.

Brunel also loved the fine Wilton carpets on the hallway and up the grand staircase. This didn't, however, mean that he bothered to wipe his shoes when he came through the front door. Instead, he walked quickly in, handed his hat to Stevenson the butler, and bounded up the stairs two at a time.

On the first floor he stopped outside the drawing room and put his head round the door to say hello to Mary, who was looking decorative and smiled nicely at him. He always looked in on Mary first – after all she was Mrs Brunel and that was what was due. And if you had asked him, he would have told you that of course he loved his wife – what man didn't? – and it was a confounded impudence of you to even posit the question. But, after a hard week's work, what Brunel really wanted was some fun, and he hadn't seen his children for days. So he bounded up the second flight of stairs to the nursery.

There were squeals of delight when he opened the door. Little Isambard, a delicate-looking boy of six with a limp, ran staggering forwards to embrace him. A smaller, sturdier little boy with long curls ambushed his knees the way that toddlers do. This was one-year-old Henry.

Brunel flung Henry in the air and caught him. He gave his older son a mock punch in the chest.

"What shall it be? A pillow fight? Bulldogs? Charades?"

Isambard II looked up at his father adoringly and whispered "Magic!"

Brunel pulled out a cambric handkerchief that had been used to wipe a piece of machinery earlier in the day. He deftly swivelled the square of cloth in his hands and made some knots. Lo and behold! Suddenly the handkerchief was a rabbit with two muddy cotton ears and a knot for a nose. The rabbit seemed to be trying to jump out of Brunel's hand and burrow down the back of young Isambard's neck, making the boy shriek with laughter. Then the rabbit bounced over onto Henry's button nose and a fat hand rose to grab it. But Henry was too slow – with a flick, the rabbit was gone and all Brunel held in his hand was a limp, muddy handkerchief.

"More papa, please. Do give us another trick!" implored young Isambard.

Brunel looked round for a minute. He was limited this evening. His magic matchbox was in the drawing room, and his cuffs were too tight for the disappearing stuffed owl trick. If only he had kept his hat on, that was always wonderful for improvising.

"Please papa, oh do!" pleaded Isambard II.

Brunel patted his body to see what he had on him. Then he opened his pocket book, and brought out a small, gold half-sovereign. "Behold this coin!" said Brunel in a fierce, gravelly voice and he held the half-sovereign up to the gaslight.

"Do the drum roll, lad!" he whispered.

Young Isambard tapped his hands rhythmically against the brass fender while Brunel continued in the same gravelly voice, "Ladies and gentlemen. This half sovereign that you see before you is about to undergo a magical process of bloodless human tissue fissure. When I say the word 'trimrumrumriddle' this coin will pass in one single flash through my brain and my thoughts and my feelings and past my ears and out through my cranium."

"Isambard, give us more drum roll!"

The child beat his hands madly against the fender. Henry joined in enthusiastically.

And now Brunel brought the half sovereign up to his lips, tilted back his throat and opened his mouth very wide. At this point he would normally press the coin down in the palm of his hand with his ring finger as he pretended to gulp it down. But maybe today he was more tired than he realised, or perhaps some of the oil and mud from the dirty handkerchief hampered his grip. Whatever the reason, the half sovereign slipped from his fingers and, as he gave a start of surprise, he felt something jolt, quickly and excruciatingly, in his throat.

He had swallowed the half-sovereign.

Brunel stood very still for a moment, feeling quite odd.

Isambard stopped drumming. "Papa, you didn't say 'trimrumrumriddle.'"

Brunel smiled weakly, "No child, something has happened. I've swallowed the coin."

"Yes?" said Isambard II expectantly.

"Well. I swallowed the coin."

"But don't you always?"

"No, child."

Isambard II looked puzzled. "So you mean, the coin's gone for ever?"

"Well maybe it will come through me. It will probably come out when I go to the lavatory."

Isambard wrinkled his nose.

"Don't worry." said Brunel gallantly. "Think of the goose that laid the golden eggs. Only I'll be better than that – I'll produce ready money."

But Brunel wasn't a golden goose and he didn't lay his half-sovereign. As the days passed, Mary got tired of asking genteelly if he had "seen" his coin yet, and

Brunel put the incident behind him and returned to his maelstrom of bridges and tunnels and railways and other projects.

He had, however, developed a cough. And after a couple of weeks the cough had become so severe that the distinguished surgeon Sir Benjamin Brodie was called in. The physician listened carefully to his chest and diagnosed the problem: that coin was stuck in Brunel's right bronchus, one of the two tubes leading from the windpipe into the lung. Dr Brodie recommended Brunel try bending down and maybe the coin would become dislodged of its own accord. Otherwise surgery was the only option – and there was no anaesthetic in 1843.

In the drawing-room the following day, with Mary and his parents sitting in attendance, Brunel bent over the seat of a chair and waited. Everyone was silent, watching him closely. Suddenly his eyes widened. The small, heavy coin had fallen forwards into his throat, where it felt as big as a peach stone. At last! Brunel staggered to his feet but, as he did so, the coin fell back down his windpipe and he was gripped by a terrible spasm of coughing.

When the coughing subsided, he tried once more. But again the coin slipped back down into the bronchus and led to another violent fit of coughing.

There had to be a better way. Brunel made a quick sketch of a hinged table with straps, pivoted between two upright poles. The apparatus was ready by 25 April and, that day, Brunel was duly strapped onto the table. He sent Mary Brunel and the children's old Irish nurse out of the room, and then the hinge was operated. Brunel gradually turned topsy turvy, with his head towards the ground and his feet in the air. Then the eminent Dr Brodie thumped on the back between the shoulder blades. The effect was as if one of Brunel's own Great Western locomotives had driven into his chest. He gasped, he choked, he spluttered, and then he coughed and coughed and coughed and couldn't ever catch his breath. With his face puce and his legs waggling desperately, he fought for air.

Dr Brodie shouted at the servants to swivel the mechanism back round again. They did so as quickly as they could and brought Brunel the right way up again. But the coughing still didn't stop, and Dr Brodie hovered ineffectually while Brunel choked and barked and hiccoughed all the more. And, as Brunel's face got redder, Dr Brodie's face became paler – for it was professional disaster to kill off a celebrity patient.

Eventually the coughing did stop and Brunel could breathe properly. A minute ago he had thought that would never be possible. What a way to die! Just like a second Saint Peter, crucified upside down.

"I'll be deuced if we do that again!" exclaimed Brunel.

He looked at Dr Brodie's gaunt face. Dr Brodie looked back at him. Dr Brodie looked at the ground. Brunel wiped his brow and sighed. Dr Brodie sighed too and shook his head sadly. Brunel knew exactly what the doctor was going to say.

The operation was to be a "tracheotomy" – when a hole is cut in the front of the throat, just below the Adam's apple. Brunel, however, needed a couple of days to recover from the coughing fit before embarking on surgery. And this break also gave him time to devise a new instrument to torture himself with. He wanted to be sure that when the doctor cut the hole in his windpipe, he would be able to get down the bronchus and extract the coin. So, to this end, he designed a special set of slender metal pincers, nearly two feet long.

On 27 April, Brodie operated. He did so in the kitchen of 18 Duke Street, for it was common in those days for people to have operations at home. As there was no anaesthetic, Brunel drank morphine in the form of laudanum drops diluted in warm water. Brunel also gave himself a slug of brandy. Then he lay down on the kitchen table and Stephenson and Brodie's assistant tied him down with leather straps to stop him moving during the operation. Dr Brodie took a scalpel and quickly made a cut three inches long across the front of Brunel's throat, just under the Adam's apple.

Even though he was expecting pain, Brunel flinched. Thus was worse than anything he had felt before, worse than anything he could have imagined. This was torture! And, what made it even worse, he had no control! He couldn't speak, he couldn't move, all he could do was watch.

The second incision was worse, for now Dr Brodie had changed scalpels and, with a sawing motion, he could was cutting through the gristle of the wind-pipe. Dr Brodie was frowning with concentration. He knew he had to be careful. Tracheotomies were not straightforward procedures. If he accidentally nicked the thyroid gland there would be blood everywhere, and then there was that cursed coughing reflex that so often got in the way. And Dr Brodie did wish that Brunel would shut his eyes and stop watching him.

Dr Brodie finished the incision and put in a clamp to keep the windpipe open. Now he took the forceps and gently eased them into the bloody hole he had made in the middle of Brunel's throat.

Just as he did so, Brunel's chest suddenly heaved with coughing. Quickly Dr Brodie tried to move the forceps further down inside his windpipe, but Brunel coughed and coughed, his chest moving up and down, the veins on his forehead throbbing and blood from the wound pouring down the sides of his his neck. The forceps, blocked by Brunel's convulsions, could go no further. It was no use. If Dr Brodie went on any longer, the treatment would kill the patient. He removed the forceps.

Eventually, the coughing subsided and Brunel was able to breathe again. Pale and exhausted, and with a gaping hole in his throat big enough to pass a golf ball, he tottered off to bed.

Five days later, Brunel lay once more on the kitchen table and Dr Brodie tired yet again with the forceps. But the coughing was even worse than before, wracking his body and blocking all breath. This time it took him eleven days to recover and muster his strength.

By now nearly six weeks had passed since the day

of the fateful conjuring trick and Brunel despaired of ever being free of the coin. But he was determined not to have the murderous forceps down his throat again. Anything would be better than that – even his old head-over-heels table.

So he resolved to try the turned-upside-down treatment one last time. And at four o'clock in the afternoon, on 13 May, 1843, his special invention was wheeled back into the sitting room at Duke Street and Brunel was again strapped onto the table top.

This time Dr Brodie was more cautious. He struck Brunel quite gently on the back and, as usual Brunel began to cough. Only the coughing was not as violent as before, and as he coughed, Brunel felt something move in his chest. He coughed a little more. And out of his mouth dropped the small shining coin.

Now that he was well, he sat down and wrote an article for the *Times* detailing all that had happened – the coin, the forceps, the head-over-heels table. Then he promptly made plans to return to Bristol by the end of the week.

There was no time to spare. Brunel was busy building Britain's industrial infrastructure and he had to oversee his ever-growing web of railways, and his countless bridges, and his locks and docks.

He also had another, new preoccupation, that would eventually dominate all his other concerns and lead to his downfall.

Brunel had started to build ships.

CHAPTER SIX
The Ships

When Brunel took to shipbuilding he, of course, made bigger, more innovative, more ambitious ships than any that had gone before. First came the *SS Great Western*, which was conceived as a continuation of the Great Western Railway for passengers who didn't want merely to travel from London to Bristol, but wished to go on all the way to New York.

In the 1830s, journeys across the Atlantic were always made in sailing ships, for it was assumed that no steam ship could carry enough fuel to power itself for the entire journey. But Brunel knew from his study of mathematics that it was merely a question of scale and proportion* and that bigger vessels used less fuel relative to their size. If only he made the ship large enough it could carry its own fuel and still have room for passengers and cargo. So he built the

SS Great Western, 236 feet long, and the largest ship in the world at the time, with engines maintaining double the steam pressure of any ship afloat.

There were other innovations. Brunel designed a special cut-off valve to limit the steam entering the engine's cylinders and so save fuel. He also reinforced the hull with extra iron and wood diagonals to withstand the currents of the Atlantic. Yet, for all its extra trussing, the *SS Great Western* wasn't an ugly boat. Carved on the elegant prow was a gilded Neptune born up by two dolphins.

On 31 March, 1838, the *SS Great Western* set out from London. She was bound for Bristol and would then embark on her first Atlantic crossing. Brunel and his friend Captain Christopher Claxton (whose son had been on the death-defying trip across the Avon Gorge) were standing on deck in the morning sunlight when they first smelled burning.

In moments the fire took hold. Flames and smoke belched out from the forward boiler room. Stokers, screaming with fear and pain, ran out of the engine room and jumped straight overboard. Soon the deck itself was on fire. Amid the smoke and confusion Claxton and Brunel lost each other. Claxton, with a fire hose in his hand, ran to the engine room, where he found the felt and leather lagging around the steam funnel was on fire. Claxton took up position under the boiler hole and directed his hose straight into the flames. Soon he was standing up to his shins in water, with clouds of smoke and steam billowing all around him.

Then, a moment later, something large and heavy hurtled down the engine hole and knocked Claxton sideways. He crawled onto all fours in the water and staggered to his feet. Through the smoke and steam, he saw what had hit him. A man's body was lying very still, face down in the water.

Claxton pulled the man's face clear of the water. Then he cupped his hands and called up the engine hole, "A rope! For God's sake!"

The flames round the boiler were gaining again, and when the rope came Claxton didn't even have time to see if the poor devil was dead or alive. He just tied the rope round the man's middle and shouted to the men to pull.

It was only later, when the fire was under control that Claxton discovered that the man who had fallen on top of him was, of course, Isambard Kingdom Brunel. The great engineer had been climbing down into the engine hole when a ladder collapsed and sent him hurtling eighteen feet down. If Claxton hadn't broken his fall and fished him out of the water, he would almost certainly have died.

But instead Brunel was just badly injured. He lay on the deck, wrapped up in a sail, and groggily muttered instructions. There was, he insisted, no need to turn back. The men must first put out the remains of the fire and then sail full steam ahead for Bristol.

Brunel himself was not fit for travel. The men lowered him onto a small boat that carried him to the little island of Canvey in the Thames estuary. Here he lay immobilised for several weeks. This didn't, however, stop him from working. Soon after the *SS Great Western* arrived in Bristol, Captain Claxton received two pages of detailed instructions which Brunel had dictated from his sick bed.

Commercially the *SS Great Western* didn't start off well. On her maiden voyage from Bristol to New York there were only seven passengers – most people having cancelled after news of the fire reached Bristol. And later the highly lucrative post office contract to carry the mail to and from America went to Edward Cunard, who ran a rival steamship company. But, as a piece of engineering, the *Great Western* was a great success. She was powerful, well proportioned and extremely strong. In eight years she crossed the Atlantic 67 times.

Brunel, unsurprisingly, wasn't satisfied. The *Great Western* hadn't completed her second voyage when he was already planning a far bigger, better and even more radically innovative ship. This ship, which would be the *SS Great Britain,* would weigh over 3,000 tons and be the largest ship in the world. Also it would be made of iron, a material that at the time had only been used on far smaller hulls.

This presented Brunel with many different and exhilarating problems. There was no shipyard geared up to build a hull this size and new machinery also had to be planned. And how could he make the ship sufficiently strong? He abandoned traditional ship-building methods and adopted a new "cellular" principle of construction, with the hull criss-crossed with girders and divided by partitions into smaller, water-tight compartments.

Trickiest of all was the business of the engine. At first Brunel wanted a traditional paddle engine, but the crank shaft would have been so large that there was no hammer in the world big enough to forge it. Then, when this problem had been overcome and the engines were already half-built, Brunel changed his mind, abandoned the paddles and opted for a screw propeller. This meant the engine had to be redesigned and remade at great speed. The subcontractor, stressed beyond endurance, came down with a fever and died shortly afterwards.

Eventually, on 19th July, 1843, the SS *Great Britain* was ready for launching. She sat in a Bristol dry dock, a great lump of a ship, with a long black hull and golden Arms of England on the bow. Prince Albert came down to Bristol in a special train. There was a banquet for 600 people. Flags fluttered, church bells rang, martial music blared, guns were fired and the crowds cheered. The sluices opened and the new ship was towed out of the dry dock into the floating harbour. Everyone went home happy.

But there was still a little problem about the size of the new ship. The locks leading from the floating harbour in Bristol out onto the mouth of the river Avon were too narrow for the SS *Great Western* to pass.

The Bristol Dock Company agreed to the temporary removal of masonry from these sidewalls, but it would only do so once an Act of Parliament had granted permission. A year and a half passed while the *SS Great Britain* waited for the Act to come through.

Finally, with high tide on 11th December, 1844, she edged out into the lock. Three quarters of the way in, her sides scraped against the walls of the lock and suddenly she jammed to a halt. Quickly Claxton and his men pulled her back into the floating harbour before the tide ebbed, leaving her beached in the mud. All day long Claxton and Brunel frantically organised workmen to move more masonry and widen the lock just a little bit more. That night, on the very last of the spring tides, the *SS Great Britain* squeezed through the lock and sailed out into the sea.

But her problems had only begun. *SS Great Britain* proved to be a fine ship and she sailed several times across the Atlantic and even did so in the record time of fourteen days and 21 hours (sailboats normally took twice as long). But on the pitch dark, rainy night of 22nd September, 1846, just hours after she had left Liverpool, disaster struck. The passengers were in their cabins for the night, when there was a terrible roar of rending metal, and the ship juddered to a halt. Poor Captain Hosken, who was in charge of the ship, had become confused because a new lighthouse was in operation and his charts were wrong. He now had no idea where he was. Had they hit the Isle of Man?

When dawn broke, the crew and passengers saw that the ship was aground in a lonely, sandy bay. Above them loomed a range of great mountains that swept straight down to the sea. This was Dundrum Bay, in County Down. They had hit the coast of Ireland.

Later that morning, little lines of Irish carts carried the bedraggled passengers and their trunks off to safety. Captain Hosken had ordered the men to throw bags of coal overboard, but without the coal and without the passengers the SS *Great Britain* still wouldn't float. Under the sand lay rocks which had pierced through the ship's hull in two places.

Five days later the SS *Great Britain* was still stuck on the rocks. A terrible gale promptly blew up and thousands of tons of water came crashing down on the ship. Captain Claxton, who happened to be on board, abandoned any hope of refloating the ship further into the bay to try to protect her from the very worst of the waves.

But even after this desperate measure, SS *Great Britain* was still taking a terrible pounding. The bay was so exposed that, unless something drastic was done, the ship would simply fall to pieces before she could be safely taken for repair in the spring.

Throughout October and November, the ship lay in the bay, being pummelled by the waves. The salvage experts came and went. They tried to construct breakwaters, but no sooner were the sea walls created than they were washed away. The Great Western Steamship Company, which owned the *SS Great Western* and *SS Great Britain* and had already suffered severe financial setbacks, seemed to have given up hope of ever salvaging her.

In December 1846, Brunel, who up until this point had been too busy with his million and one other projects to come to Ireland, finally arrived in Dundrum Bay. It was what the Irish call a "soft" day: grey skies, bleak light, drizzle. But Brunel wasn't bothered – his top hat and his rage kept him warm. For there in front of him, lying all grim and grubby and lopsided in the water, was his ship – the biggest, fastest, best steam ship in the world.

There was not, he noted, even *one* breakwater in operation. *SS Great Britain* was completely unprotected. All that was wrong with this fine ship was a few holes in the bottom and slight damage to the stern. Otherwise she was straight and sound as ever. And she had been left here to moulder like an old saucepan on Brighton Beach. These schemers and underwriters had just abandoned her! It was positively cruel!

Brunel paced up and down the beach. He waded out into the bay, scowling hard at the hull and chewing on his cigar. The freezing water swirled around his trouser bottoms. No wonder the breakwaters had all washed away! Nothing, except this enormous ship, could remain firm against these currents...

Then the idea came to him. And, like all really good ideas, it was so obvious, and so very simple: he would use the ship itself to form the breakwater.

He took out a pencil and a small notebook and, as the rain splattered slowly onto the paper, he drew what he had in mind: the beached *SS Great Britain*, with something resembling a thatch covering the stern and one side of the hull. This huge barrier, which was to be propped up against the ship, was to be built from piles of brushwood bound together and then skewered with iron rods. These bundles would be lashed into place with iron chains and weighted down with iron blocks and sand bags.

Brunel scratched out some calculations down the

side of the page. It wouldn't take much. He would need to bring in a few hundred tons of iron for the rods and as much again for the lengths of chain. But there was plenty of forestry in the local estates and the Irish always needed work. Captain Claxton could surely charm the local landowners and commandeer a few carts. A mere £4,000 or £5,000 was all that would be needed. Without waiting for permission from the Great Western Steamship Company, Brunel started carrying out his plan. Then, having chided and galvanised everyone into action, he returned to London.

His great friend Captain Claxton supervised the rescue operation. Through the spring of 1847, carts creaked across the strand, carrying piles of brush-wood for the gigantic barrier. At first, despite Brunel's ingenious plan, the piles of brushwood still kept being washed away. Claxton wrote to Brunel about his problems with the piles, or "fagots" of brushwood.

He received a fierce reply: "You have failed... from that which causes nine-tenths of failures in this world – by not doing enough. If a six-bundle fagot won't reach out of the water, try a twenty-bundle one. If hundred-weights won't keep it down, try tons."

Claxton struggled on. Many, many fagots later,

he finally established a firm footing for the barrier. When the ship was at last sheltered from the waves, the hull was raised and the holes temporarily patched up.

All sorts of other mishaps followed, but finally, on 28th August, 1847, a very waterlogged *SS Great Britain*, was towed into Coburg Dock in Liverpool to be repaired. The *SS Great Britain* had been saved, but the entire undertaking, from the building of the barrier to the journey back across the Irish Sea, had been beset with difficulties.

And the cost was vast. The Great Western Steam-ship Company now faced financial ruin and went into liquidation. The company's two ships, *SS Great Western* and *SS Great Britain*, were sold on.

But Brunel, of course, was undeterred. He wanted to build an even bigger ship. Amazingly, he could still find the financial backers.

CHAPTER SEVEN
"The Leviathon"

Although Brunel was still configuring the railways of southern England and building a brace of bridges, he as usual made time for his hobby horses. And in 1852, as he sketched designs for his Italianate villa outside Torquay and rearranged the trees and landscape round about it, his plans for his next big creation began to take shape.

This was to be what he called his "great ship". It was to have six masts, five funnels, ten boilers, two sets of engines, with both paddle-wheel and screw propeller propulsion, and two entire iron hulls, one inside the other and with a three-foot gap in between. Above all, the ship was to be absolutely enormous – six times the size of anything else afloat at the time and too big for any existing harbour. Brunel envisaged the ship carrying 4,000 passengers.

There was a reason for the vast proportions. Gold had been discovered in Australia in 1851 and trade with the colony was booming. Brunel wanted to build a ship with such a capacity that it could make the journey to Australia without the trouble and expense of having to stop to refuel.

And, of course, Brunel loved a challenge. With the railways, he felt he couldn't do much. Since the boom, speculators and accountants had taken over. These businessmen were only interested in money. They had no sense of grandeur and lacked finesse. He also suspected that they did not care about the advancement of engineering. But shipping, well that was another matter... And a really big ship would be such a magnificent monument to the age.

Getting the initial funding for the ship proved to be the least of Brunel's problems. In early 1852, with the help of Captain Claxton and the shipbuilder John Scott Russell, he had managed to interest some of the directors of the newly formed Eastern Steam Navigation Company in building a gigantic ship. Brunel was most compelling and soon had himself appointed as chief engineer. Some of the directors, who were nervous of the ship and probably nervous of Brunel, resigned. They were promptly replaced by Brunel's nominees. By 1854, £120,000 had been drummed up – Brunel himself took out 2,000 shares in the company – and work began.

Brunel's new ship was built on the banks of the River Thames at the Isle of Dogs in London. This was a desolate spot – an evil-smelling stretch of black water backing on to shipyards and flat marshy fields edged with rows of crooked cottages and pubs. Against this miserable backdrop, the great ship gradually rose up. The hull, which was 60 feet high, came to dominate the skyline (remember London had no skyscrapers then). The little houses, and the pubs, were all dwarfed by this looming black cliff of iron.

People began to call the ship "the Leviathon", meaning "gigantic sea monster". The men working on the hull seemed like ants. Like ants, there were many of them – more than 2,000 shipbuilders were employed. And also like ants, they worked astonishingly hard. For, despite the Victorian's glorious breakthroughs in engineering, many working practices remained relatively unchanged.

Brunel poo-pooed the idea of building a crane, so the workmen climbed up to the decks on wooden towers and hauled up thousands of tons of iron on pulleys. And there were no forklift trucks, so the heavy iron plates that made up the hull were trundled around the site on wheelbarrows. These iron plates were held in place by some three million rivets*, each of which was hammered in by hand. The red-hot rivet would be thrown by a relay of boys to a riveter and his "closer up", who would take turns to hammer the metal flat. Meanwhile, on the other side – in the hot, hellish gap between the two hulls – another work-man, with a boy to help him, would hold the rivet in place.

The riveters and the apprentices worked twelve hour days, six days a week, down in the dark between the reverberating hulls. The idea of such a terrible existence probably spooked people. And it is said that one riveter and his boy became trapped between the hulls and were left to die. Years later, when the ship was finally broken up, so the story goes, the skeletons of a man and a boy were discovered.

It is true that workmen were killed during the construction of the great ship, including a boy who fell and was impaled on an iron bar where his dying body twitched horribly. But the trapped riveter and his boy are most probably a myth, and there is no evidence whatsoever that skeletons were later found. However, this tale – and the very fact that people

were talking of hauntings and trapped skeletons –
does point to a larger truth. "The Leviathon" was
an unhappy, unlucky ship. And, from the very start,
things began to go wrong.

For Brunel there were two main problems. The first
was his health. From the early 1850s onwards he
was not a well man. He had pains in his chest and
suffered fevers and fatigue. His hands and feet would
swell up and on a bad day he could look as jowly
as a walrus. His skin would feel horribly itchy. He
had outbreaks of nausea and in his mouth there was
a curious metallic taste. When he went to the bath-
room, his urine was sometimes the colour of well-
brewed tea.

The symptoms were many and varied – for Brunel
was suffering from the early stages of kidney failure.
He didn't know this yet; he just called his ailments
his "concatenation of evils" and whenever possible
he kept on working at his usual furious pace. But one
thing was constant – he felt absolutely dreadful. And
it didn't improve his temper.

Brunel's other problem, which probably gave him
more grief than his failing health, was the fact that
for once in his life he was not completely in charge

of everything and everybody. This gigantic whale of a ship was Brunel's greatest brainchild. It was his dream, the project he loved above all others. Here he had staked his reputation and much of his personal fortune.

The trouble was that ships were not Brunel's forte. He knew about bridges and railways and tunnels. But of naval architecture and shipbuilding he had relatively little experience. So, from the start, he had teamed up with John Scott Russell, who was probably the foremost shipbuilder of his day. The idea was that while Brunel would be chief engineer and in sole command, Russell and his men would be responsible for drawing up the detailed plans and constructing the ship.

This would have been a fine arrangement, were it not for the fact that the two men had completely different working styles. Russell was accustomed to delegating: and Brunel wanted to check and second-guess everything personally. Brunel was also a perfectionist, he was continually dissatisfied. While Russell and his team started to erect the ship, Brunel continued to alter the plans, dithering and redesigning and double-checking and asking for more figures and engine tests. During construction he changed the positions of the screw propeller and the paddle boxes. He decided to raise the height of the deck once it had already been riveted into place.

So, with these changes and queries, construction was delayed. There were other problems: weather, inflation, and two fires in Russell's shipyard that cost the shipbuilder tens of thousands of pounds. Brunel became impatient. He claimed that his queries were not answered, that Russell was "disorganised" and that tons of iron had gone missing in the yard. He wrote ferocious notes to Russell and started docking and blocking his payments. By 1856, Russell was all but bankrupt and for three months work on the ship came to a complete standstill.

But the ship, despite all these boardroom wranglings, did eventually get built – with Russell taking a back seat for a while in proceedings. And finally, in late 1857, she was ready to be launched.

All London had watched the great monster grow on the banks of the Thames and many had wondered how Brunel would get her into the water. The great engineer, always keen to try out novel ideas, had set his heart on doing a sideways controlled launch – slipping the ship gradually into the Thames with the help of hydraulic rams* and enormous winches and brakes. This method had never been used before and Russell, who had launched hundreds of ships, advised against it. But Brunel insisted on doing it his way.

So the launch of this ship was really a gigantic and dangerous experiment. Brunel applied himself to the problem for months, calibrating, calculating and carrying out mini-experiments. He eventually decided to use more than one method at once. He placed a hydraulic ram at the bow* and stern*, and then had huge lengths of chain running from the ship onto four winches on barges moored out in the river. In case the ship moved too fast, Brunel had also ordered two twenty-foot brake drums, which stood at either end of the ship. For that was the real danger. If the ship didn't move at all (which was very likely) then Brunel could always apply more force. But should she slide out of control... Well, that didn't bear thinking about.

Because of all the problems and delays with the building of the ship, there wasn't any time to test these moorings or the chain tackles. But there was one thing Brunel knew to be vital: all the rams and drums and winches had to be perfectly coordinated. So, as there weren't loud speakers or radios in those days, Brunel devised an elaborate system of red and white flags. He would stand on his raised platform and direct operations.

It was, of course, vital that everyone be alert, and able to concentrate fully on the task at hand. Peace and calm must reign in the shipyard. There should be as few distractions as possible, and, of course, no unnecessary visitors. Brunel drafted stern instructions to his staff. "Nothing", he wrote, "is more important than perfect silence."

But the directors of the Eastern Steam Navigation Company had other ideas. Soon Brunel discovered, to his horror, that the company were selling tickets to the launch and that over 3,000 people were paying to enter the yard. Others followed suit. Makeshift grandstands started to appear. Local pubs put out flags and hired brass bands.

The launch, it seemed, was to be a great spectacle and a grand day out. The citizens of London had watched "the Leviathon" grow to its astonishing size – now they would witness its first plunge into the water.

And there was always the possibility that something would go terribly wrong: for 10,000 tons of this ship (that is the weight of 1,667 elephants) had to slide down the bank of the Thames and into the water. Nobody wanted to is the opportunity for such an almighty catastrophe.

On the morning of 3rd November, 1857, everybody came to the launch: shopkeepers and lawyers, servants and housewives, shop girls with their skirts hitched up over their woollen stockings, tradesmen in overalls, bank clerks, cart drivers, cockle-sellers and newspaper boys, pickpockets and shipyard navvies, black-faced stokers and elegant ladies in bonnets and kid gloves. The Comte de Paris came and so, too, did the Duke of Amale. The Siamese Ambassador brought a wonderful retinue dressed in turbans and printed cotton trousers. How the urchins gawped.

The crowd was raucous and excited. Onlookers swarmed around the hull and the big checking drums. Children scuttled everywhere. Four constables, hired by the yard to keep the crowd in order, charged hither and thither grabbing drunks and yelling at the public to keep off the equipment. Several brass bands blared away – most were out of tune as the players were already drunk. And always there was the thud of sledgehammers – as the shipyard workers knocked away the wooden wedges holding the ship in place. So much for Brunel's "perfect silence".

By midday, the wedges were all out. Brunel stood at the foot of the rostrum with his head pounding and his nerves in tatters. His shirt was grimy round the collar. He hadn't dressed for the occasion. How could he? He hadn't been home for days.

Now it was time for the launch. Brunel took a deep breath and was just starting to mount the wooden steps, when someone grabbed at his coat sleeve. He turned to see John Yates, the company secretary, smiling apologetically and holding out a piece of paper. Yates had been responsible for selling the tickets to the public and Brunel still felt so angry that he could barely look at the man.

"Well sir?" asked Brunel brushing at his sleeve.

Yates had to shout to make himself heard. "I'll warrant you're busy, Mr Brunel, but we still have no name and Miss Hope is waiting. I have the directors' proposals here." Yates proffered the piece of paper, but Brunel shook his head.

Yates tried again: "What do you say to 'The Leviathon'? That's a fine sounding name. Or 'The Great Eastern'?"

Brunel moved his gaze from his sleeves to the grey skies above. He spoke sharply, "You'll call her 'Tom Thumb' for all I care!"

Then he turned and walked up the steps. He heard the cheer as Miss Hope, the chairman's daughter, broke a bottle of champagne over the hull and named the ship *The Leviathon*. In fact, this wasn't to become the ship's official name – the directors later changed their minds and registered her as the the *SS Great Eastern*.

Anyway, at the time, the naming of the ship seemed an irrelevance. Brunel's mind was on other matters. That day, at 12.25pm, he stood at the front of the rostrum, blinked slowly and gave a slight bow. He waited for the roar of the mob to die down. His "perfect silence" never came but, after a constable blew his whistle, there was a distinct quietening of the crowd.

Brunel raised the white flag to slacken off the cables on the checking drums. He ordered the barges out on the river to take the strain on their chains and then, with another wave of the white flag, the teams down below cranked the steam winches into action.

Brunel gave the signal to the men to heave hard. Nothing seemed to happen, and the ship wasn't moving. A strange low rumbling noise, like a roll of drums, filled the air. Brunel waited. The rumbling went on and on. He knew it was the sound of the chains pulled tight and reverberating against the iron hull, but it did add to the suspense. How long would they have to wait? Was it his imagining or was that sound getting louder? Would the ship ever move?

Brunel fumbled in his waistcoat and brought out his watch. Ten minutes had gone past. It was time to try more force. Brunel waved his white flags and the hydraulic rams were put into action.

The effect was instant. There was a shout and the ground shook. And, with a sudden jerk, the whole front of the ship slid three feet down the bank. The team on the forward checking drums quickly yanked the brake lever, and the ship stopped.

But the men out in the barges, so terrified by the great hull juddering towards them, abandoned their winches. Then the ground shook again and this time the stern of the ship jerked forward. Terrible screams came from near the brake drum. Up above the heads of the crowd flew the limp body of an old man.

Sometimes, during the most terrible accidents, events happen at a strangely drawn out pace – as though life itself were pausing to take breath. And so, even though the old man sped through the air, it seemed as if he went very slowly. And Brunel, watching him in horror, could see that the old man did not look right. His feet were mangled. His legs were all bent in the wrong places, as if they had been put on the wrong way round. Indeed he was so limp he could have been a rag doll – were it not for all the blood. And he hurtled along so very slowly, dying as he flew through the air.

Just for once the crowd was silent.

After the accident, Brunel suspended operations. The old man, who had been resting on a winch handle when it spun out of control, died. Several others were also injured. Eventually, the disgruntled crowd went home.

It was to take another three months to launch the ship. "The Leviathon" – or the "Leave-Her-High-and-Dryathon" as she was nicknamed – stood on the bank of the Thames all through the murky, freezing days of November and December 1857 and into the equally murky, freezing days of January 1858. Brunel faced every sort of problem: from frozen pipes to broken machinery and weak links in the huge chains around the ship's hull. He worried about the high winds and the terrible weather of that winter and he kept watch over the tides minute by minute. At times he lived on board the ship and barely slept.

But eventually, over several weeks and with the help of 21 hydraulic rams, he slid the huge black bulk down into the Thames. And on 31st January, 1858, at 1.42 in the morning (Brunel of course, noted the time precisely), the *SS Great Eastern* finally floated in the water. This time there had been no spectators and no brass bands.

The ship, however, was far from finished. She needed rigging and furnishings and engines fitted. For most of 1858, nothing happened: the Eastern Steam Navigation Company had run out of money. And, after the stress and sleeplessness of the launch, Brunel's health was in ruins.

His doctors ordered him to rest, which Brunel did with characteristic vigour, by travelling to Europe and taking with him the designs he was working on for the Eastern Bengal Railway. First he went to the spa town of Vichy in France, then he toured the Swiss Alps, and then, for the final leg of the trip, he dropped in on the Netherlands.

In September, Brunel returned to England but he still felt terrible and was wobbly on his feet. Two months later, the ESN Company, which was now bankrupt, folded and in its place came the newly created Great Ship Company which brought a fresh injection of funds.

A new contract was drawn up and given to John Scott Russell. Brunel would dearly have loved to be in charge of the work. But his health was no better than before and Sir Benjamin Brodie – his faithful doctor from the days of the gold half sovereign – ordered him to go to Egypt for the winter.

Brunel did so, accompanied by Mary, his second son Henry, a physician, and vast quantities of luggage. The rest cure, like the last one, was vigorous. In the Mediterranean, his ship met a storm and while his family lay retching with seasickness in their bunks down below, Brunel the invalid stayed wedged in a corner of the deck noting down the wind velocity, the number of turns of the paddle wheel and the time interval between each wave.

By Christmas, the Brunels had reached Cairo and they dined there one night with the great engineer Robert Stephenson, who was also incurably ill. The Brunels then took a boat up the Nile and, when they reached Luxor, Brunel and young Henry explored Karnak and the Valley of the Kings on donkeys. By February, they were down in Aswan where Brunel alighted on the idea of ascending the cataracts.

For this adventure he bought a small wooden date boat, hired local labourers and had the boat fitted with three cabins. There followed a lively trip up the rapids.

On the return journey, the Brunels visited Naples and Rome, and eventually returned to London in May 1859. Brunel was by now a spent force – pale and frail and wracked with internal pains. The Royal Albert Bridge, which he had designed, had been completed. He was taken to see the bridge but was so weak that he had to be carried on a couch.

But there were days when he could walk. And then he would hobble on his stick down to the *SS Great Eastern*, which was now nearing completion. On board, workmen thronged every deck and passageway. So, too, did crowds of visitors who had paid to inspect the ship and who pointed and asked questions and let the children play chase along the passageways.

Amid this chaos Brunel tried to reassert his old control and wandered around checking details. On days when he was confined to his bed, he dictated endless letters.

He had a view on everything: the cabin fittings, the best coal to use, the rubber ring joints for the iron masts. Not everyone took heed. Russell and Brunel had never really resolved their differences and the workforce was divided into two camps. A sour atmosphere presided over the ship.

But the work continued apace. By early August the grand saloon had been furnished in all its gothic finery: white and gold walls, a maroon carpet, red plush chairs. The huge funnel that passed through the middle of the room was encased in gilt mirrors and panels decorated with arabesques and cherubs. Now it was time to have the customary banquet for grandees, and on 8 August Russell presided over a splendid meal to celebrate the new ship. Brunel was too ill to come.

Later in the month his health rallied and he moved into a rented house so as to be all the nearer to his beloved ship. Brunel was absolutely determined to go on the SS *Great Eastern*'s maiden voyage. He chose his cabin, which had a rocking-chair and a Turkish carpet and a sofa which, if you lifted up the seat, turned into a bath with hot and cold taps.

On 5th September, 1859, Brunel came aboard the ship, accompanied by a servant carrying his traveling case. The *Great Eastern* was due to set sail the following day and down below decks chaos reigned.

While workmen were still finishing off the cabins and kitchens, the ship was being loaded up. Porters were rolling in barrels filled with crockery and the grand saloon was piled high with furniture and bedding.

Brunel, looking terribly withered and ill, pottered around the ship. He witnessed the final dock trial of the engines and nodded blearily. Then, very slowly and carefully, he walked up onto the deck. By one of the massive funnels, he stopped to have his picture taken and removed his hat, revealing a pale, bald pate.

It was now an effort for Brunel to stand upright, but he stayed still for photographer. His head hurt and he felt so tired. He wouldn't be sure about those engines until they had had a good six hours running at sea. He felt so tired, so very, very tired.

After the photographer had finished, Brunel's legs crumpled and he collapsed on the ground. When they carried him off the ship, he was paralysed and couldn't speak, but his eyes were open.

Brunel was taken home. He had suffered a stroke, which meant there had been damage to his brain caused by a leak or a blockage in his blood vessels. Now he lay upstairs on his death bed, waiting for news of his great ship.

Everything on board the *Great Eastern* seemed to

be going relatively well. The ship left her mooring on the 7th September and two days later she was gliding along the English Channel. But then she too, like her creator, suffered a sort of stroke. For, in the grand saloon, behind the fancy panelling, pressure was building up in the water heater around the funnel.

At five minutes past six in the evening, when the passengers were already in the dining-room or up on the deck, a terrible crashing roar reverberated round the ship. The water heater in the grand saloon had exploded. The entire front of the deck rose up and the forward funnel shot into the air like a rocket. A shower of broken ironmongery and splinters fell back onto the ship. Then everything on deck was hidden in a great rush of smoke and steam.

But worse was to come. For pressurised, scalding steam had blasted the stokers down in one of the engine rooms. Now these horribly burnt men staggered out onto the deck.

One man, screaming in agony, jumped overboard but became caught up in the huge paddle wheel where his body was mangled. A passenger, seeing one of the stokers emerge from the steam, caught the man by the arm: the flesh came away in his hand.

Five men died from the explosion, and down in the

grand saloon the chandeliers and gilt mirrors were shattered into thousands of pieces. But the structure of the ship had not been affected and the Great Estern kept going and arrived in Weymouth the next day.

Back in London, Brunel was told of the disaster. But there was nothing he could do now. He was far too ill to leave his bed and, perhaps for the very first time ever in his life, he couldn't rouse himself to send out even an angry letter. For days he lay in his bedroom, drifting in and out of consciousness. Finally, on the afternoon of 15th September, 1859, he called to each member of his family in turn and spoke to them. As evening closed in, he died.

EPILOGUE

Brunel was buried in Kensal Green Cemetery on 20th September, 1859. He was only 53 at the time of his death, but he left behind him an astonishing legacy.

The Great Western Railway line from London to Bristol is possibly his greatest achievement. But countless other Brunel bridges and viaducts and tunnels and railway buildings are still in use today. Some of these, such as Paddington Station or the Royal Albert Bridge in London, you may have used without noticing. And the Thames Tunnel, which Brunel worked on with his father, is now just another part of the London Underground.

Only one of the Brunel's ships survives today. The *SS Great Britain* had a long and varied career and became a regular passenger ship to and from

Australia, until she was deemed unseaworthy and was left to rot in the Falkland Islands. In 1970 the ship – by then a splendid rusting hulk with cormorants nesting in her hull – was finally towed back to Bristol, where she was restored and is now on show.

Brunel's beloved white elephant, SS *Great Eastern*, fared less well. The ship continued just as it had started out – losing extraordinary quantities of money and being bedevilled by bad luck. (Her first captain drowned, and his replacement suffered a nervous breakdown; the grand saloon was trashed for a second time in a storm; an engine fitter had his hand ripped off by the paddle engine; and so it went on...) The ship had a brief period of fame when she was used for a new telegraph cable across the Atlantic, but she ended her days as a showboat on the Mersey in Liverpool. Here her hull became a huge advertising hoarding with the state rooms given over to restaurants and fairground attractions, acrobats using the masts and rigging for their trapeze.

Brunel's most famous construction, the Clifton Suspension Bridge, was not completed until after his death. In 1860 a group of engineers banded together to raise funds for the project in memory of their colleague. The bridge that now stands across the Clifton George, although startlingly beautiful, is in fact a pale shadow of Brunel's original design. For reasons of economy, the suspension towers are shorter and do not include Brunel's original decorations. Sadly, there are no sphinxes.

GLOSSARY

Bow – the front part of a ship, or boat

Hull – the frame, or body of a ship

Hansom cab – a small, two-wheeled, horse-drawn carriage used as a taxi

Hydraulic ram – a pulling machine, with a piston

Marsh gas – methane, an odourless, colourless, inflammable gas

Pleurisy – inflammation of the pleura, a delicate tissue that covers the lungs and lines the chest

Scale and proportion – for those who understand maths: the carrying capacity of a ship's hull increases as the cube of its dimensions, while its water resistance increases only by the square of those same dimensions

Rivet – a bolt with a head at one end, used to join two or more pieces of metal

Stern – the back of a ship, or boat

KEY DATES

1806 Isambard Kingdom Brunel is born

1825 Work begins on the Thames tunnel

1828 Brunel nearly drowns in the Thames tunnel flooding

1835 Work begins on the Great Western Railway

1836 Brunel marries Mary Horsley

1836 Foundation stone laid for the Clifton Suspension Bridge

1838 Fire aboard *SS Great Western* nearly kills Brunel

1841 First train runs on the Great Western Railway from London to Bristol

1843 The gold half sovereign stuck down Brunel's throat finally comes out

1843 *SS Great Britain* is launched

1846 *SS Great Britain* is wrecked off the coast of Ireland

1854 Work begins on *SS Great Eastern*

1858 *SS Great Eastern* finally floats

1859 Brunel suffers a stroke

1859 Explosion aboard *SS Great Eastern*

1859 Brunel dies at home

1859 Brunel is buried in Kensal Green Cemetery

QUIZ

1. Marc Brunel made his young son practise drawing...
   a) Suspension bridges
   b) Naked women
   c) Perfect circles

2. What inspired Isambard's father to invent a tunnelling machine?
   a) The Greek myth of Orpheus and Eurydice
   b) The tool his wife used to inject rum into the Christmas cake
   c) A species of worm that burrowed into ships

3. To celebrate the decision to build a tunnel under the Thames, a model was made out of:
   a) Matchsticks
   b) Sugar
   c) Lego

4. How did Isambard try to recover his health after being injured in the Thames tunnel accident of 1828?
   a) He visited Brighton and went out to parties and the theatre a lot

b) He hired a personal trainer to visit him at home three times a week

c) He consumed large quantities of Vitamin C daily

5. The Brunels hoped that their invention, the Gaz machine, would be an alternative to:
   a) Wind and water mills
   b) Steam engines
   c) Washing machines

6. When Mary Brunel went for a walk in the park, she always took:
   a) Her manservant
   b) Her pet rabbit
   c) Her mobile phone

7. Who gave permission for the London to Bristol railway to be built?
   a) The Queen
   b) Parliament
   c) Mary Brunel

8. Why were the masters of Eton College opposed to the Great Western Railway?
   a) Because they wanted to promote cycling as a healthy and ecologically sound method of travel

b) Because they didn't want the boys to be able to get up to mischief in London

c) Because many of them were Scottish and they wanted the line to go North–South rather than East–West

9. Brunel invented a new wrought iron railway track in the shape of:
   a) An upside-down U
   b) A flattened Y
   c) A horizontal W

10. At what speed did the first GWR trains travel in 1838?
   a) 25 mph
   b) 45 mph
   c) 85 mph

11. To congratulate the foreman in charge of the digging of the tunnel through Box Hill, Brunel:
   a) Gave him his very own ring
   b) Presented him with shares in the company
   c) Arranged for a fire-eater to attend his leaving party

12. The special word that Brunel said when performing magic tricks for his children was:
   a) Fiddlebottomupsadaisy

b) Trimrumrumriddle

c) Diddleydoodahcalloocallay

13. In the mid-19th century, surgical operations usually took place in:
    a) Well-equipped hospitals run by local charities
    b) Horse-drawn mobile operating theatres
    c) The patient's own kitchen

14. Once Brunel had recovered from his awful experience with the swallowed coin, he:
    a) Swore that henceforth he would pay for everything by credit card
    b) Decided to write an article about every detail for the *Times*
    c) Insisted that the family only ate puréed food for a year

15. On the prow of the *SS Great Western* was a carving of:
    a) Neptune supported by two dolphins
    b) Isambard Brunel with his arms round his two boys
    c) John Wayne riding two sea-horses

16. How many passengers did the *SS Great Western* carry on her maiden voyage?
    a) 700

b) 70

c) 7

17. What problem did the *SS Great Britain* encounter as soon as she was launched?
   a) Aeroplanes were invented and no one wanted to travel by sea any more
   b) She was too big to get out of the harbour and had to remain in Bristol Dock for 18 months
   c) Brunel found that he had forgotten to include ensuite bathrooms in the first class cabins

18. In 1852, the Isle of Dogs in East London was:
   a) A charming collection of picturesque cottages, each with a rose-covered kennel
   b) An evil-smelling, desolate area of shipyards and marshy fields
   c) A lively tourist destination with fantastic night-clubs

19. Brunel wanted perfect silence for the launch of "The Leviathon". What happened?
   a) The police made sure that the public was kept well away
   b) The directors of the company sold 3,000 tickets so people could come and watch
   c) All the workmen were required to wear earmuffs

20. Brunel's cabin on the maiden voyage of the *Great Eastern* had a sofa that converted into:

    a) A bath

    b) A sunbed

    c) A pinball machine

Answers: 1 c), 2 c), 3 b), 4 a), 5 b), 6 a), 7 b), 8 b), 9 a), 10 b), 11 a), 12 b), 13 c), 14 b), 15 a), 16 c), 17 b), 18 b), 19 b), 20 a)

Amanda Mitchison is a children's writer and journalist. She has worked as a feature writer for the *Independent Magazine* and the *Sunday Telegraph*. Amanda has published four historical biographies for children and two novels as well as a pet care guide to looking after dragons. Amanda lives near Bristol with her husband and two sons.

OTHER TITLES IN THE GREAT VICTORIANS SERIES: